patti smith
dream of life

by steven sebring

RIZZOLI
NEW YORK

When I was a teenager...

...I dreamed of being an opera singer like Maria Callas, or a jazz singer like June Christy or Chris Connor, or...

...approaching songs with a kind of mystical lethargy of Billie Holiday, or championing the downtrodden like Lotte Lenya. But...

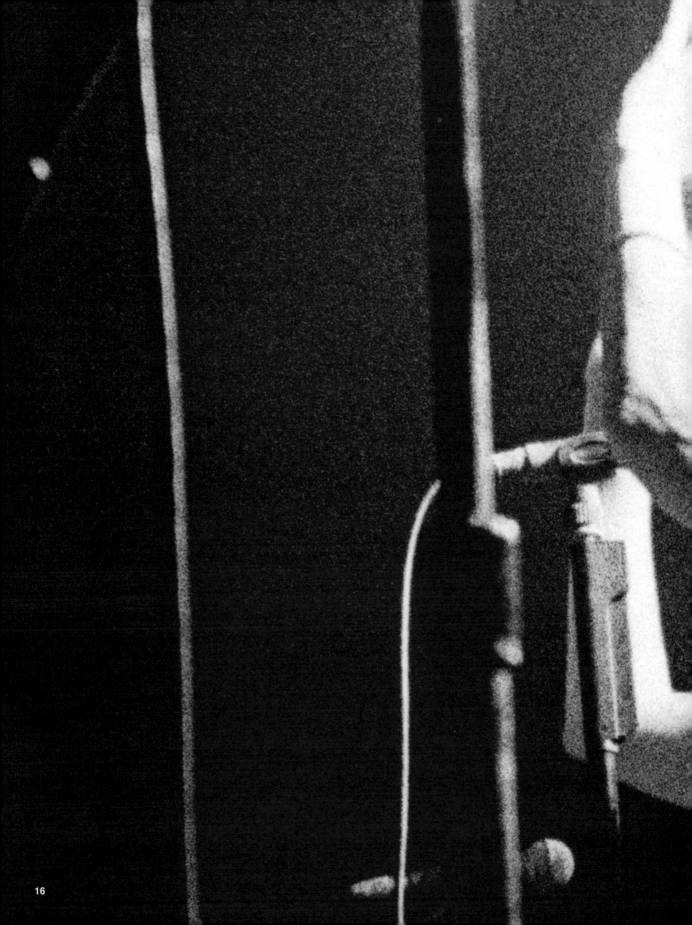

...I never dreamed of singing
in a rock 'n roll band. This idea...

...it just didn't really exist in my world. But...

...my world, as it's been said,
was "rapidly changin'."

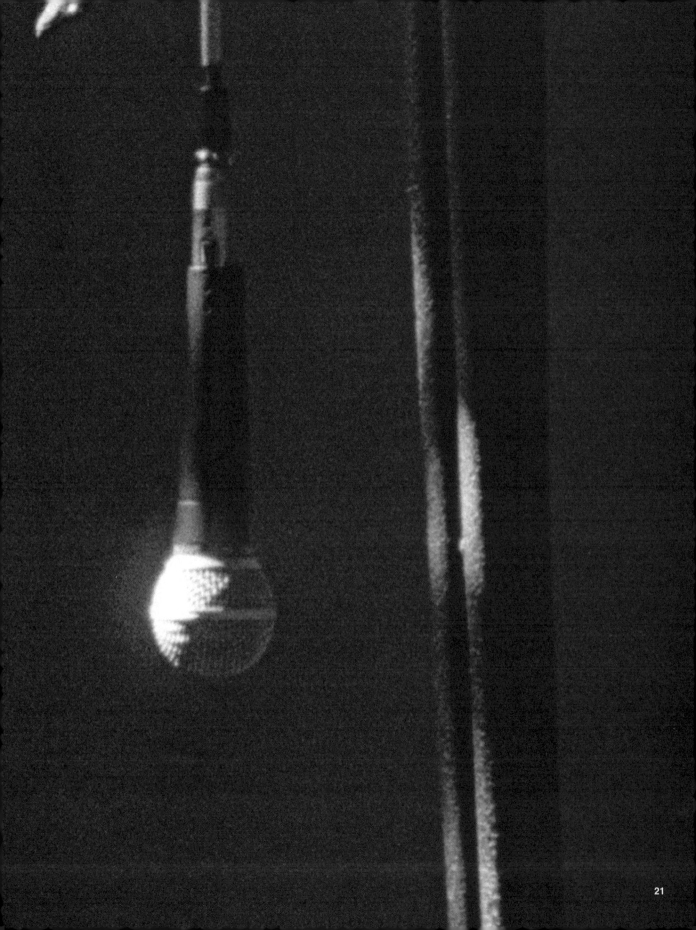

I found a fairyland right inside myself here, 'cause it let me. When I lived in South Jersey or whatever, there was no... no time for day dreaming. And life was simpler there. You weren't hassled, you didn't have people trying to hold you up or goose you and stuff like that. But that's all there was. There was no chance for extension. There was no chance to be destroyed or really be created there. Just lived, and that's okay for some people, but I always felt something different stirring in me, and that's what... that's like why I came here, 'cause I knew there was stuff inside me that... that could like flower. Maybe it would really ruin me. Maybe I'd feel really shitty about it. But at least it would come out.

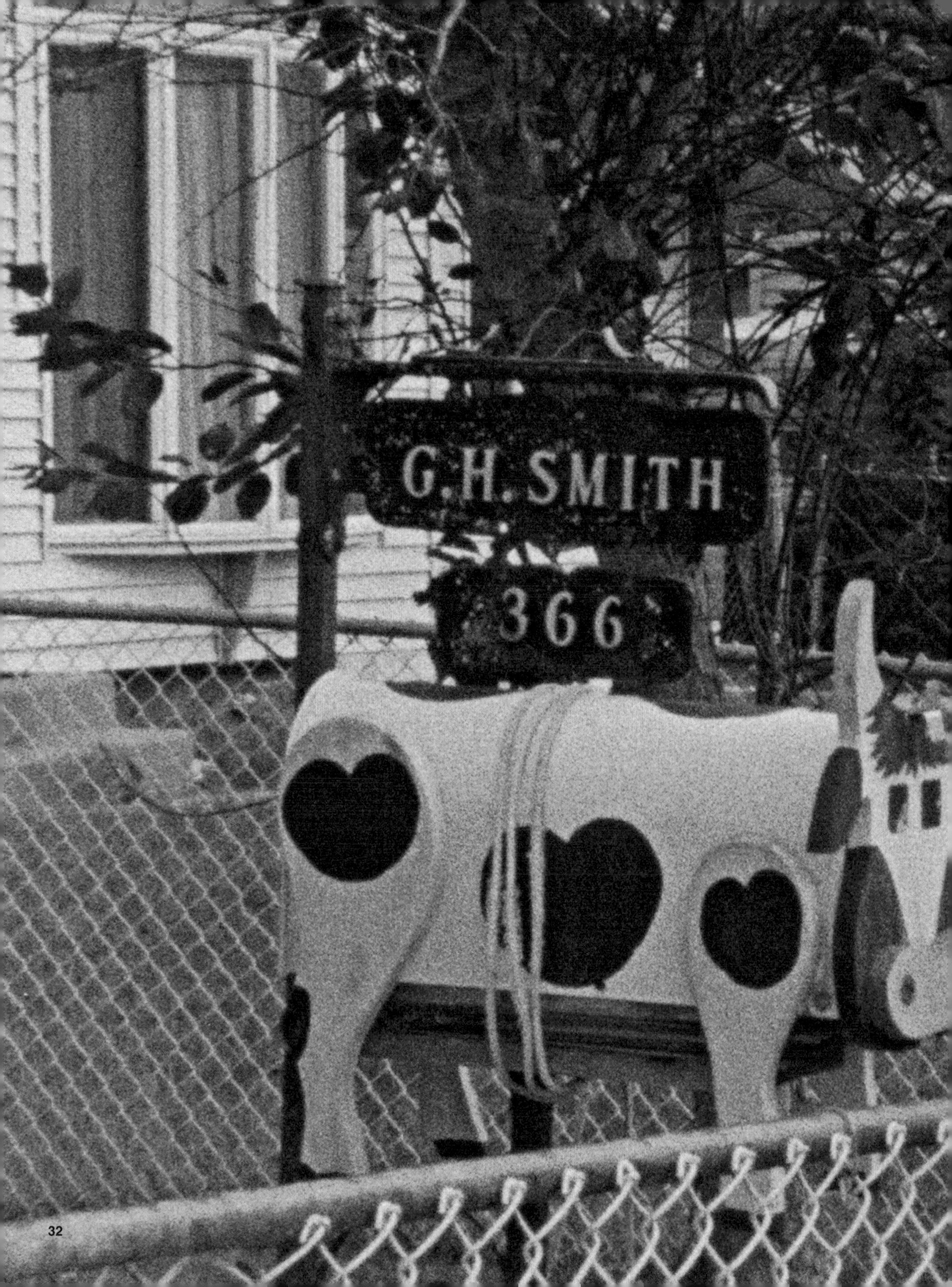
G.H. SMITH
366

PATTI SMITH: Did you plant that tree too?
DAD: No, I think that just grew by itself. But that was all right with me because I wanted a tree anyway.

We didn't have much when we were kids.
My parents worked really hard, but we had
a happy childhood.

There were always books in our house.
My mother taught me to read those books:
The Pilgrim's Progress, *Pinocchio*, and the poems
of William Blake *Songs of Innocence*.

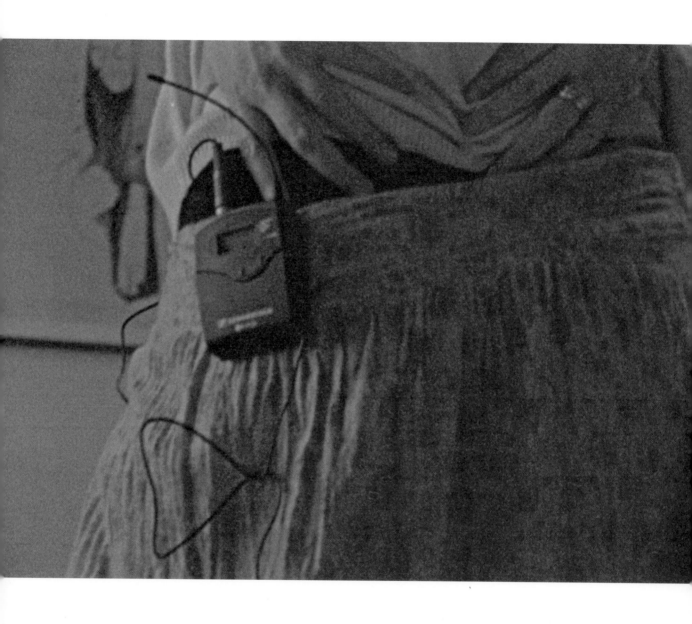

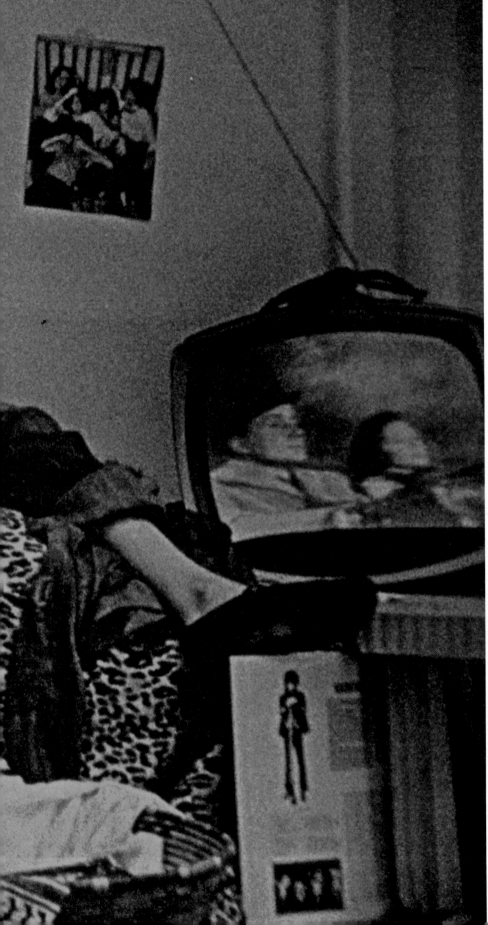

I was living at the Chelsea Hotel, and I had to wait until I met musicians and then ask them if they would...I'd say, "Oh, want to see a really cool guitar," and they'd see it and they'd go, "That's a great guitar." They'd go to play it, and I'd say, "Want to play it?" And of course they'd... they'd tune it up, and then they'd play it, and I'd get my guitar tuned. And once, even Bob Dylan himself tuned this guitar, in 1975. And he really, he said, "Hey, nice guitar." And it is.

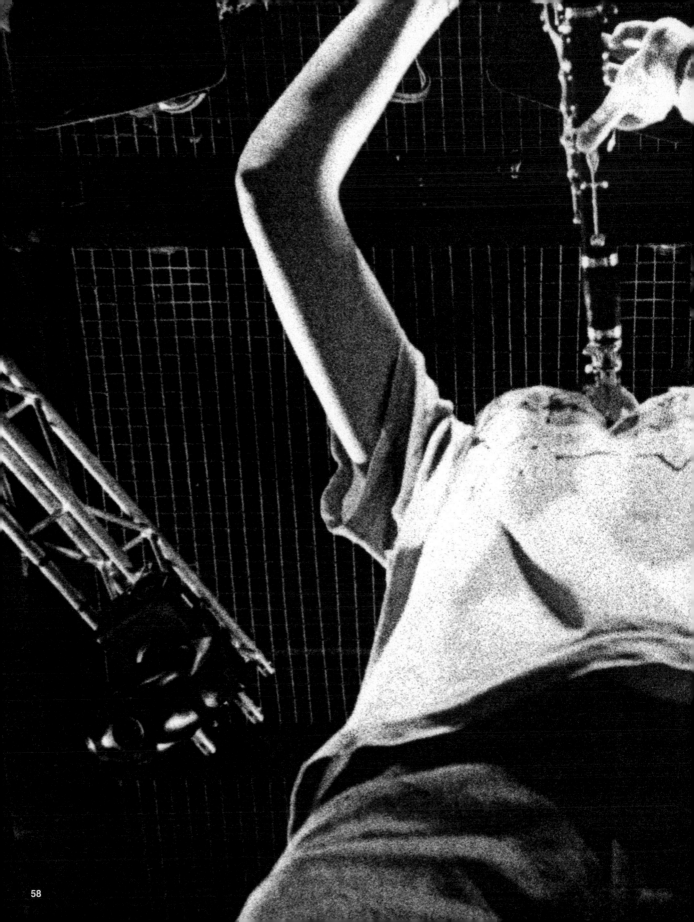

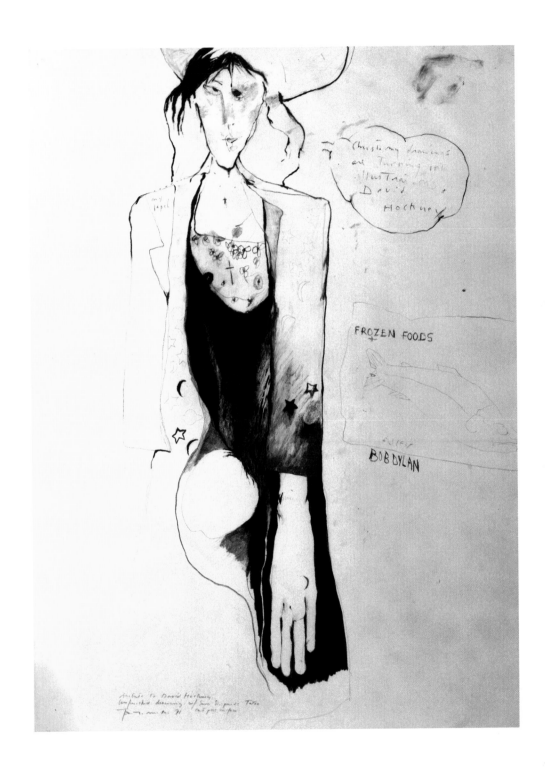

You look at somebody like Walt Whitman
who wrote, wrote in his writing
I...young poet, young poet
who will exist a hundred years from now,
I am writing for you.
I am thinking about you as I'm looking at this river.
I'm thinking about you, young poet not even born,
as I'm looking at the sky,
and our ancestors in that way thought of us,
and we in kind can think of them, and it keeps the whole...
it keeps everything rolling.

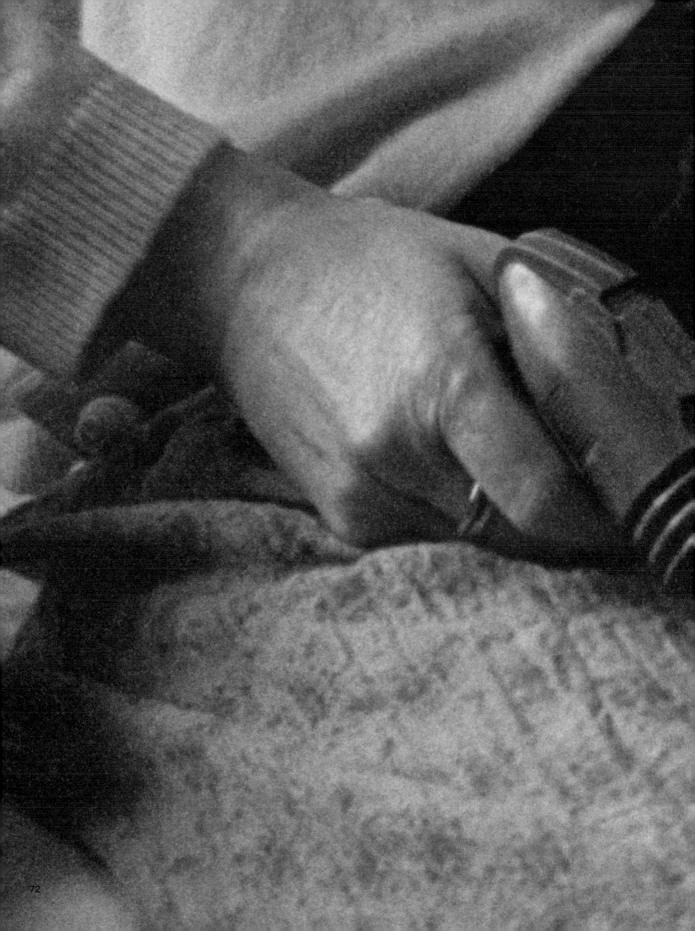

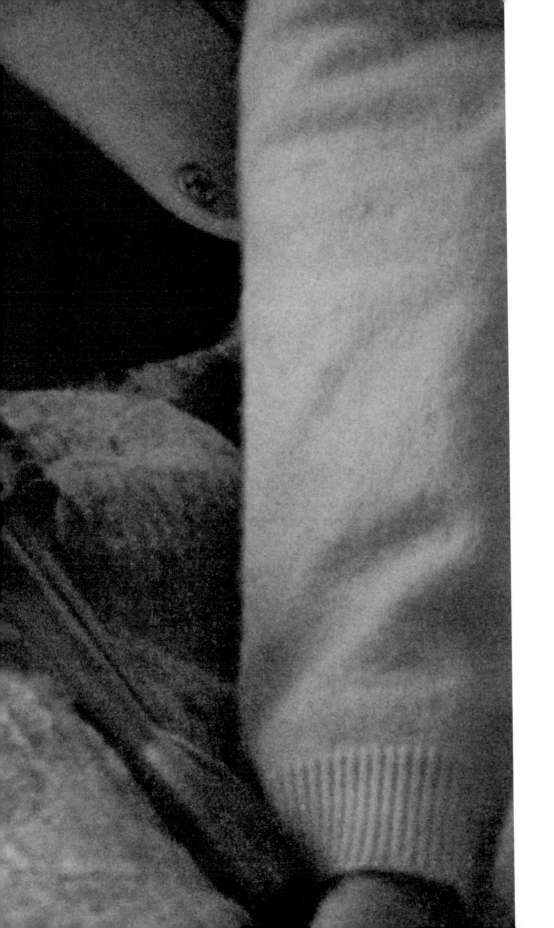

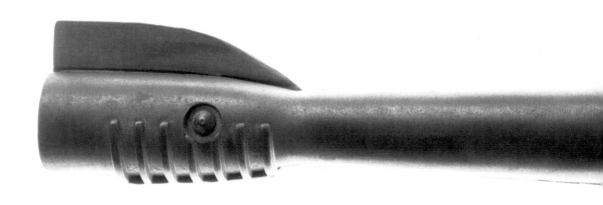

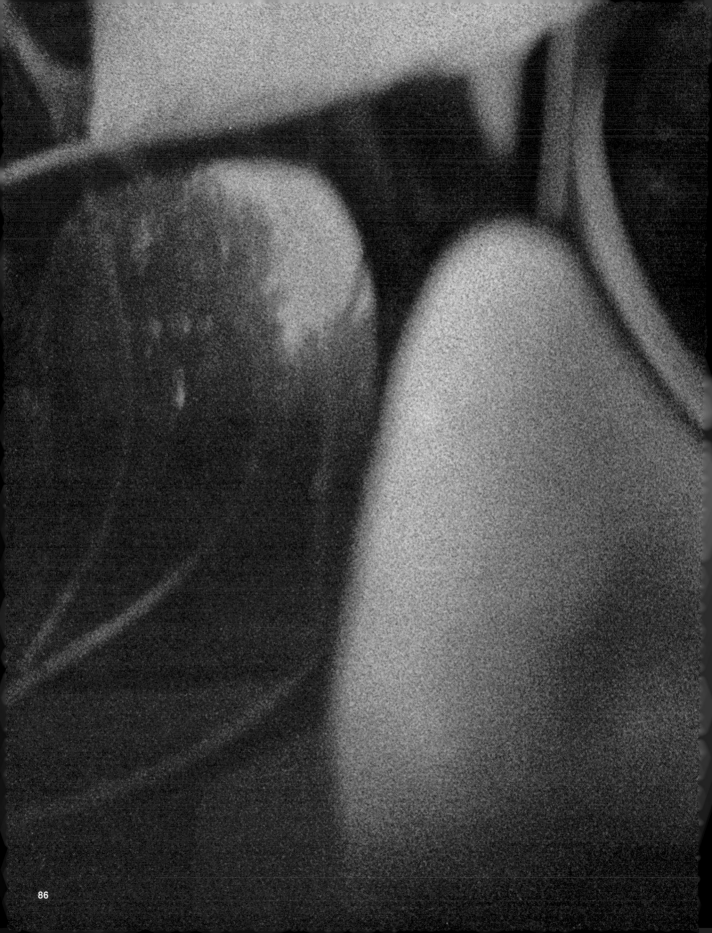

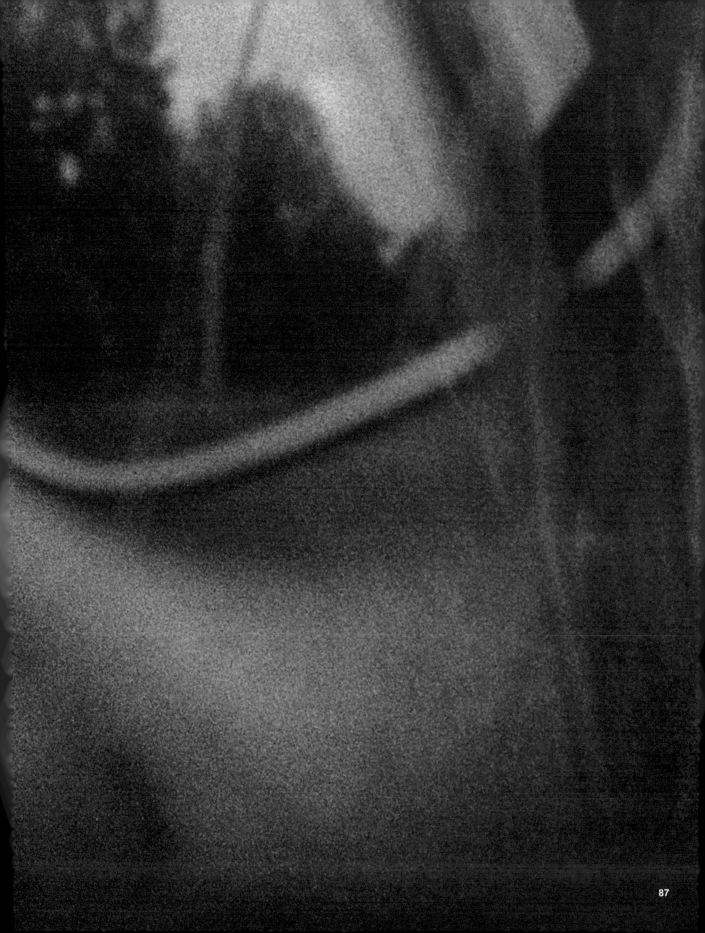

I had not performed for sixteen years. And now alone, friends and mentors offered me a hand. Bob Dylan counseled me to return and sing for the people, and we gathered our musical forces and joined him on tour. Lenny at the helm, J.D. my drummer, Tony, Oliver, and Tom Verlaine. Michael Stipe joined our caravan, offering his unconditional support. This was a joyful time of comradeship, shaking off the performance dust, of saying hello to the road and goodbye to Benjamin Smoke who passed away the year following our concert in Georgia.

Fred never saw Jackson and Jesse grow,
but I know his spirit is always with them.
And they have within them
his musicianship, his proud and dignified manner,
his stoic-ness, and when I...
when I play with Jack, I remember truly
what it tasted like to play with Fred.
Jackson's a little taller but...he fills his father's shoes.

28/29/30/31st

be a gathering

patti smith

j. c. daugherty   lenny kaye   oliver ray   tony shanahan

peace and noise

the new album.

rolling stone

CBGB

october
28/29/30/31st

be a gathering

patti smithp

l.d. daugherty   lenny kaye   oliver ray   tony shanahan   j.d.

peace and noisepe

the new album.

★★★★

rolling stone

CBGR

The mind of a child is like a kiss on the forehead,
open and disinterested.
It turns as the ballerina turns
atop a party cake with frosted tears poisonous and sweet.
A child mystified by the commonplace,
moves effortlessly into the strange
until the nakedness frightens, confounds, and he sits
and seeks a bit of cover, order. He glimpses,
he gleans, piecing together a crazy quilt of truths,
wild and bullied moments,
hardly bordering in the mind.
A vague pirouette snatches bits of code,
Flemish, hieroglyph,
embedded in the brick, chiseled in the brick,
exclamations, questions of origin, scope.
When young, overcome with a sense
of being from somewhere else, we peer, we probe inside
and pull out, alien, indian, we come upon an open plane,
a plane of gold.
We come most often upon a cloud...cloud dwellers.

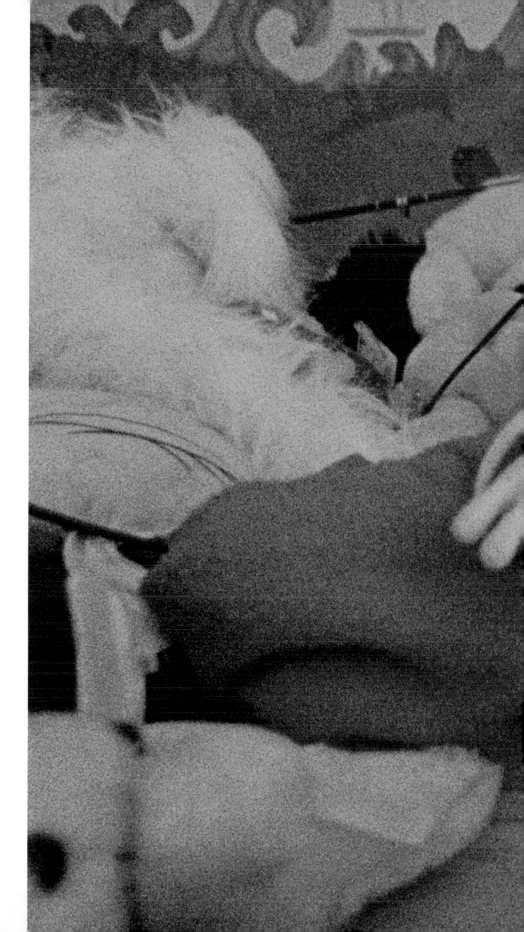

My mission is to communicate, to wake people up, to give them my energy and accept theirs. We're all in it together, and I respond emotionally as a worker, a mother, an artist, a human being with a voice. We all have a voice. We have the responsibility to exercise it, to use it.

119

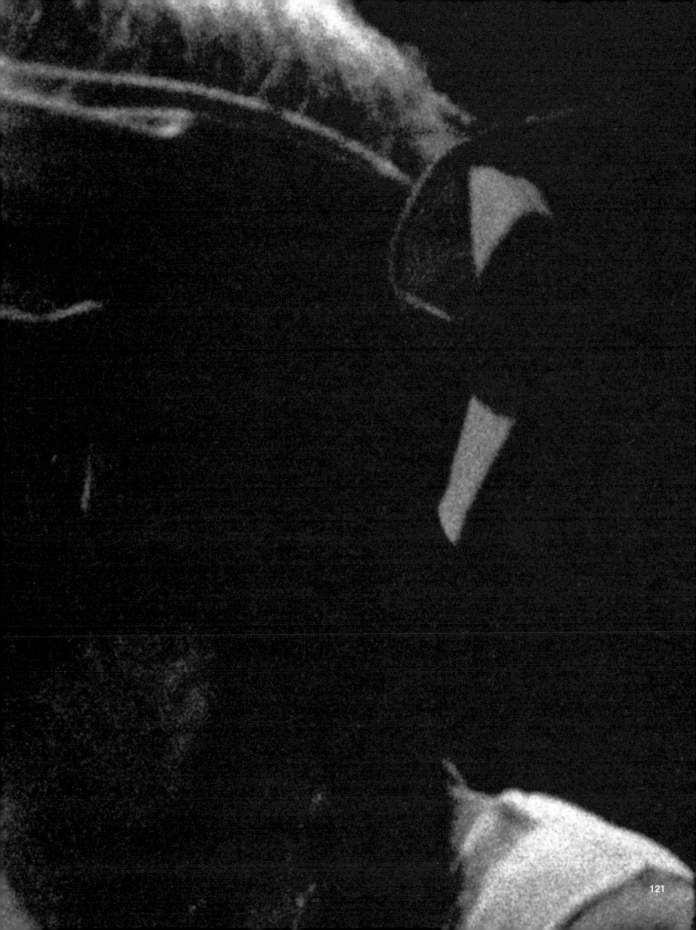

122

After Fred passed away, Allen Ginsberg
called to offer his condolences
with these words,
"Let go of the spirit of the departed, and
continue your life's celebration."

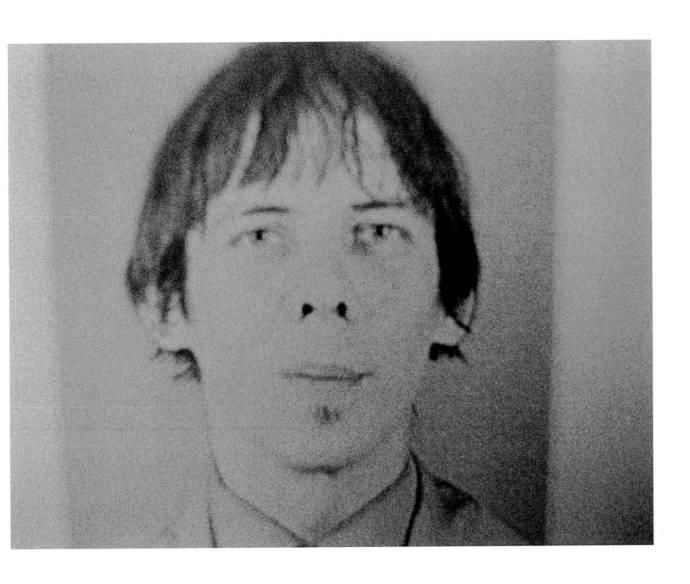

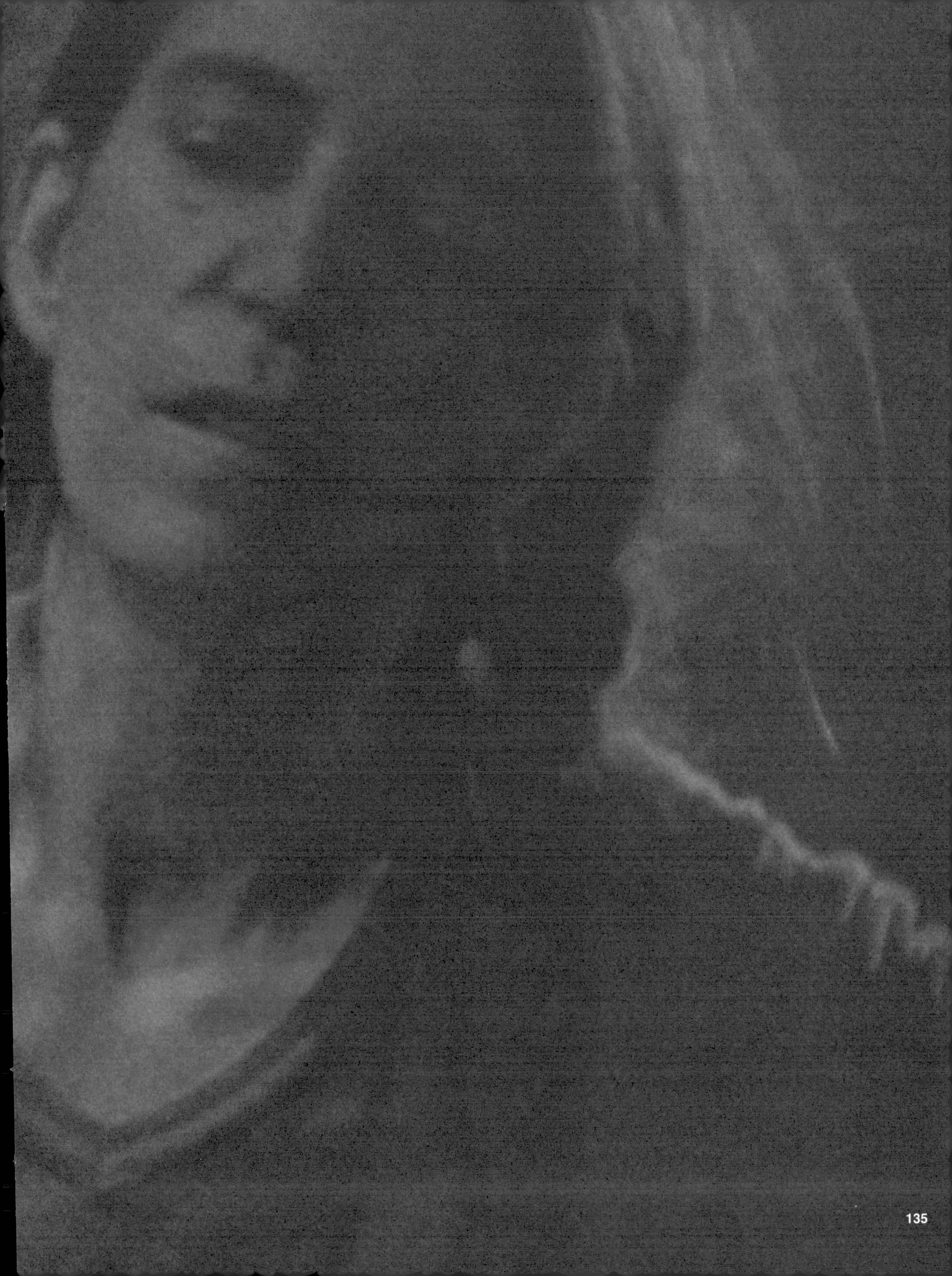

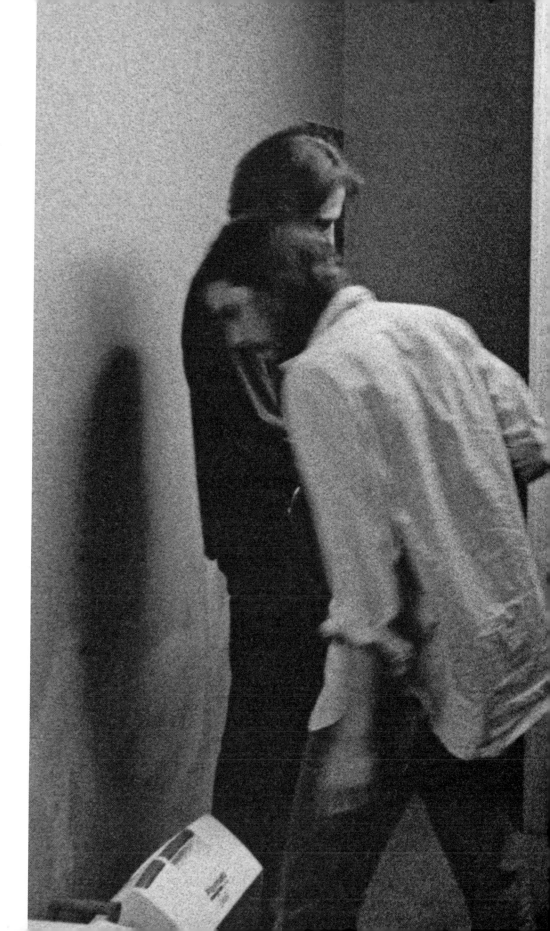

143

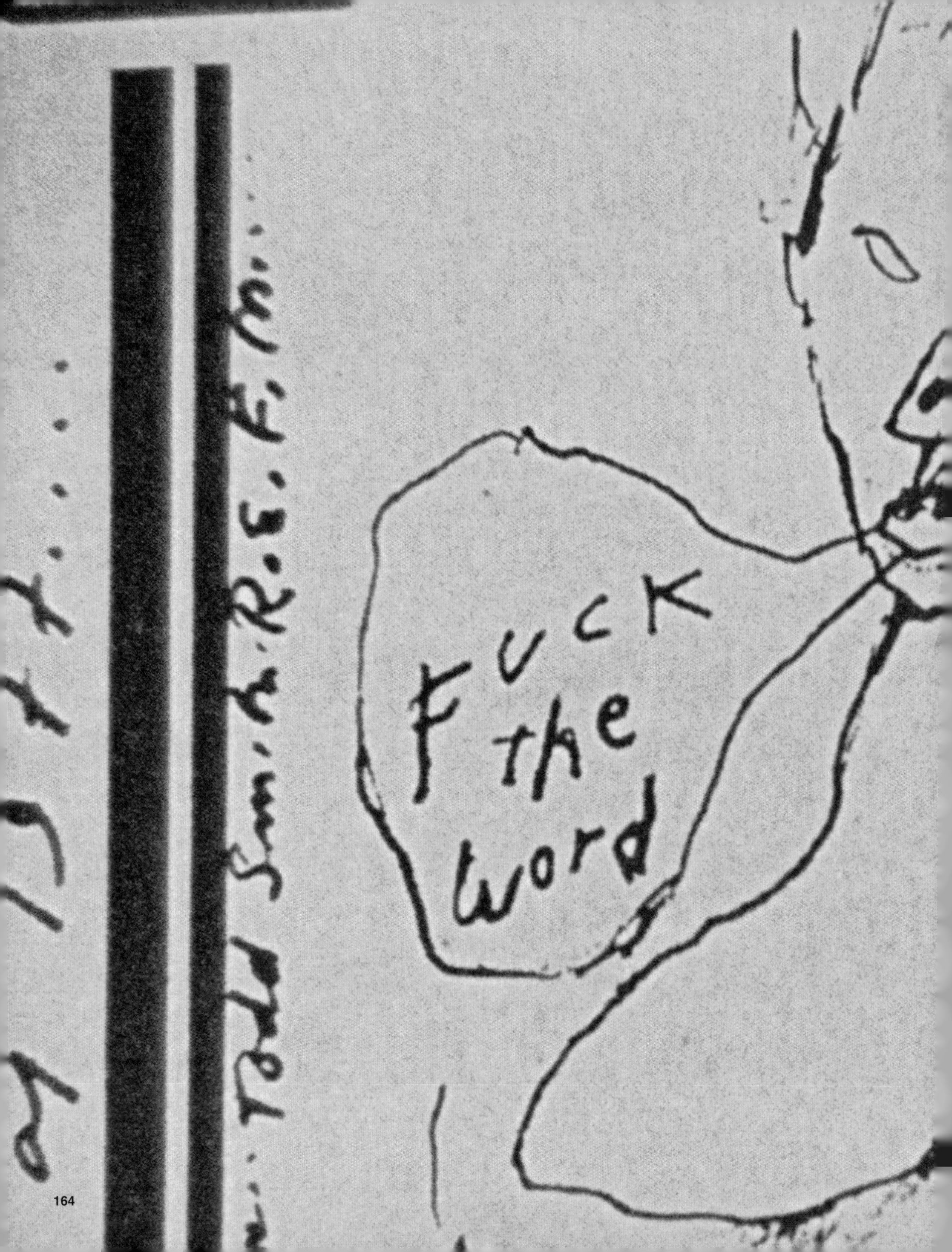
FUCK
the
word

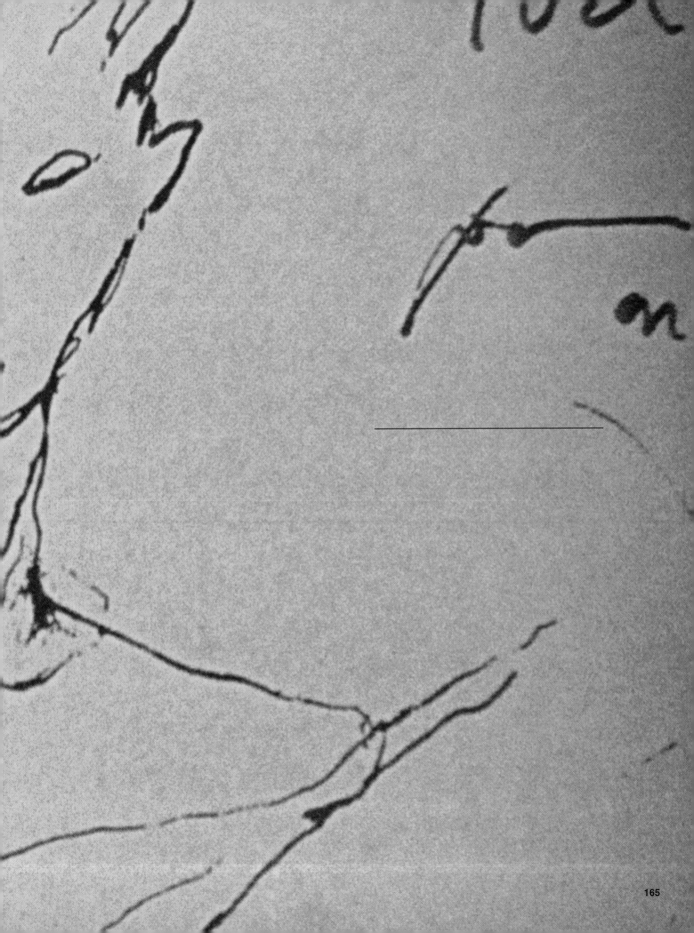

In the spring of 1994
I wrote a little song
when Jackie Kennedy
died. I read that when
she was told she was
dying, she took one
last walk by herself
through Central Park.
Fred was taken with it,
and often sang and
played it himself with
Jesse playing at his
feet. Fred's health
deteriorated that year,
and we spent less
time writing songs.
Instead, he would have
me sit and practice
the chords he taught me
and we'd end with him
singing, "She Walked
Home." Fred and I
never recorded again,
for he passed away in
November. I did not have
the heart to record
"She Walked Home"
somehow Fred had
made it his own.

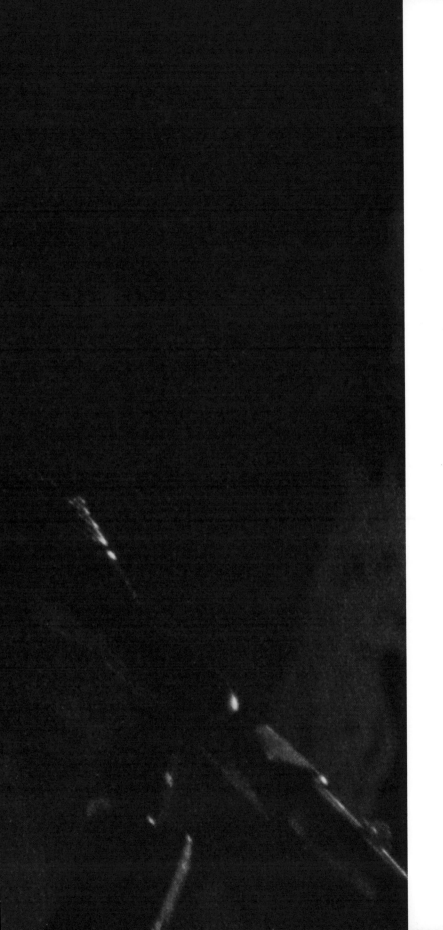

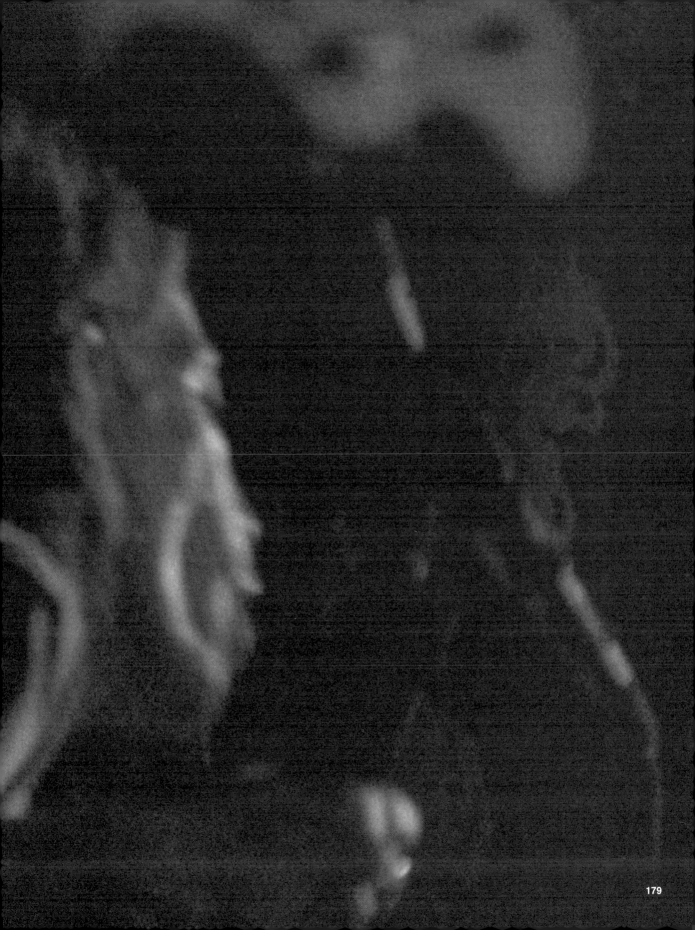

New York is the thing
that seduced me.
New York is the thing
that formed me.
New York is the thing
that deformed me.
New York is the thing
that perverted me.
New York is the thing
that converted me.
And New York is the
thing I love, too.
Yeah, it's my little
prayer for New York.

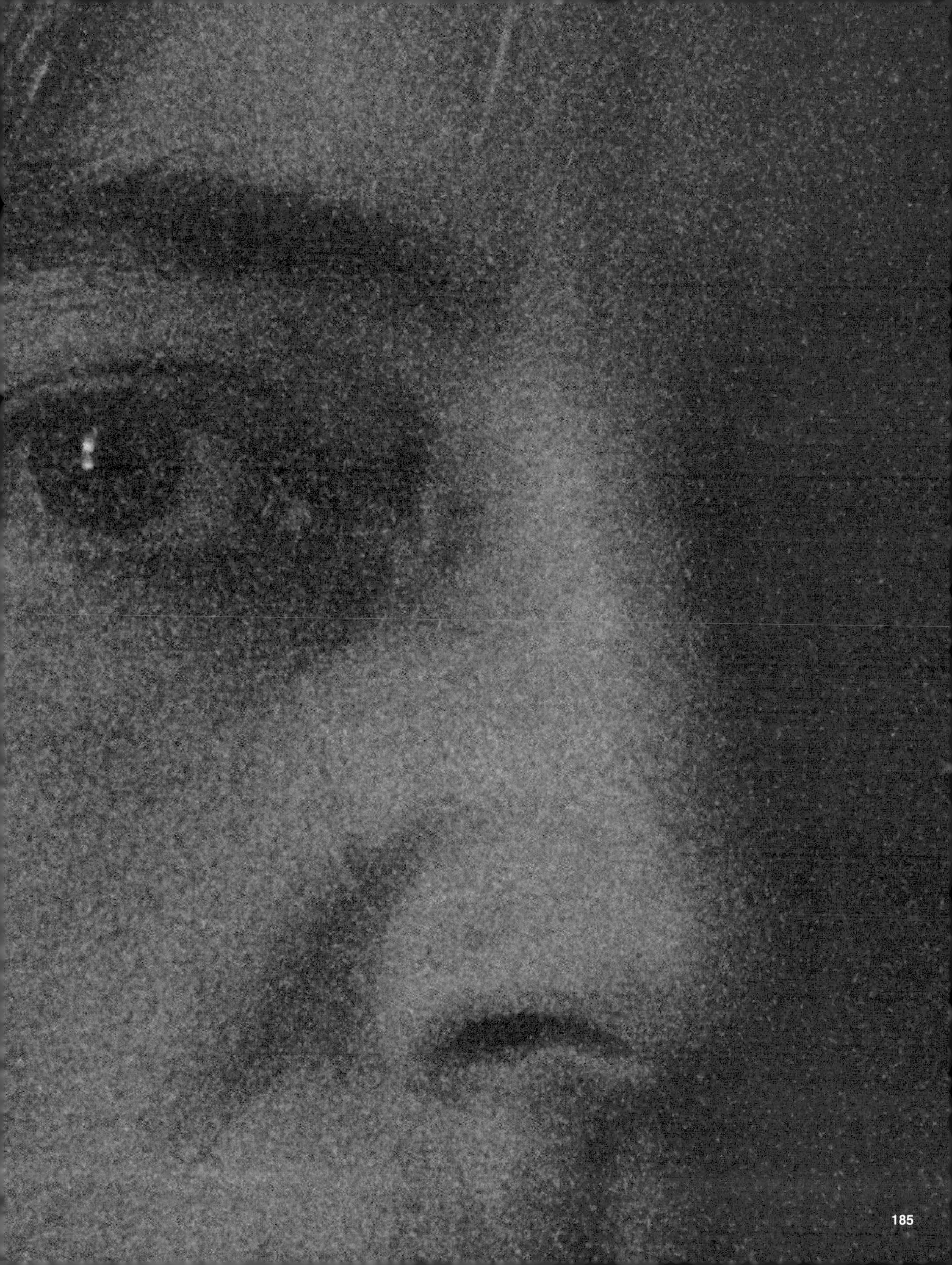

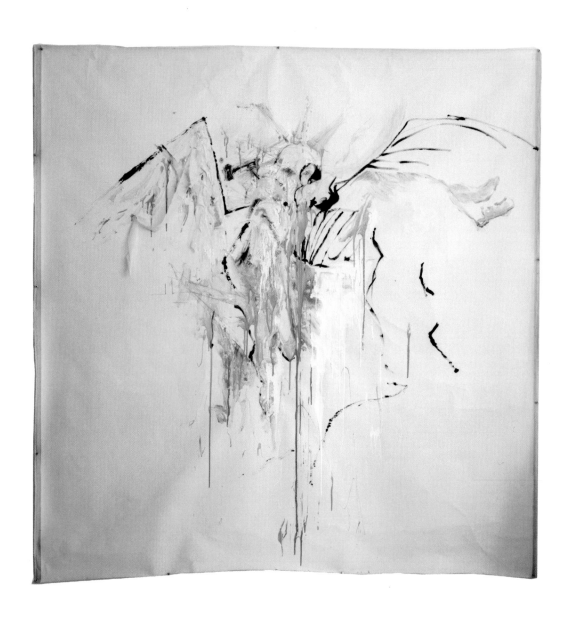

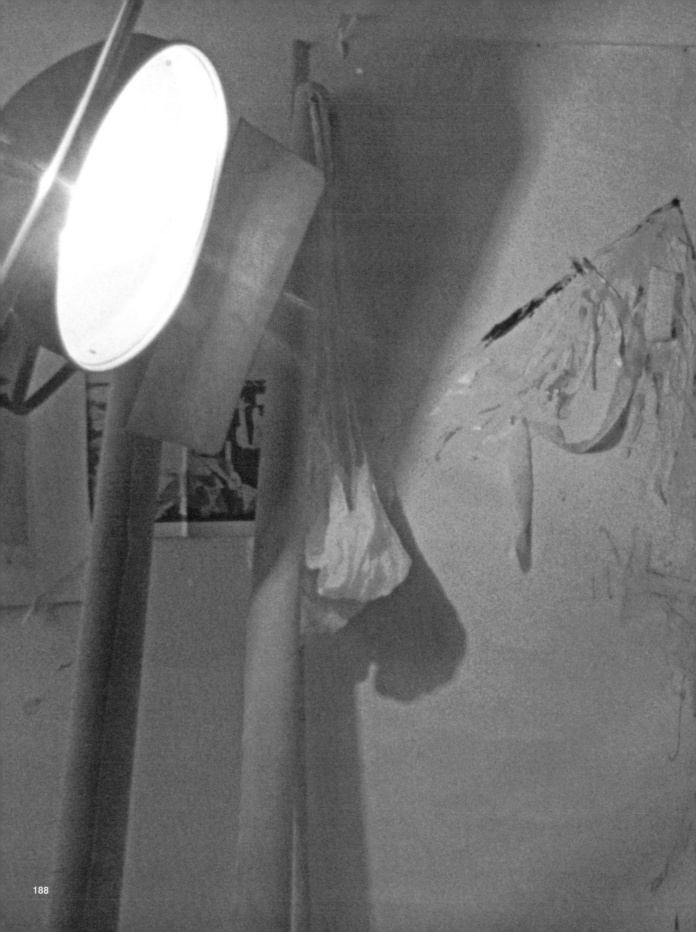

I like the story of Jackson Pollock.
Jackson Pollock was looking at a book about...
well, I guess, reproductions of Picassos and he says,
"Damn him." He like throws the book, and he says,
"Damn him, he's done it all."
Of course Picasso did do it all, except for what
Jackson Pollock did. Jackson Pollock took the drip from
the teeth of *Guernica*, the teeth of the horse from *Guernica*,
there's one horse that has just little drips of...
it might be, you know Picasso isn't one for drips,
it might be the...they're the only drips that I'm really familiar
with in Picasso's work.
It's like Jackson took the drips from the mouth of the horse
and then took that small aspect and created a new vocabulary,
a new, very American work of art.
The joy of moving through the process of discovery
belongs to every new artist, or as T.S. Eliot said,
"Every generation translates for itself,"
and it's up to us to both embrace history and break it apart,
blow it up even.
But uh anyway (*laughs*)...sorry.
I like to feel the skin of canvas.
I know it's not right to touch paintings, you know when
you go in museums. The first time I got yelled at
I was a teenager, touching a Modigliani,
I just had to feel the texture or the...just the way the paint...
de Kooning...I...
it's like I almost have to put mittens on.
You know like when you have chicken pox, you know you
cover up your hands, and so you don't scratch yourself
and make little scars?
That's how I feel looking at de Kooning...de Kooning's paintings,
that I should have little cloth mittens on.
But of course if one does one's own, then you can touch it
all you like.

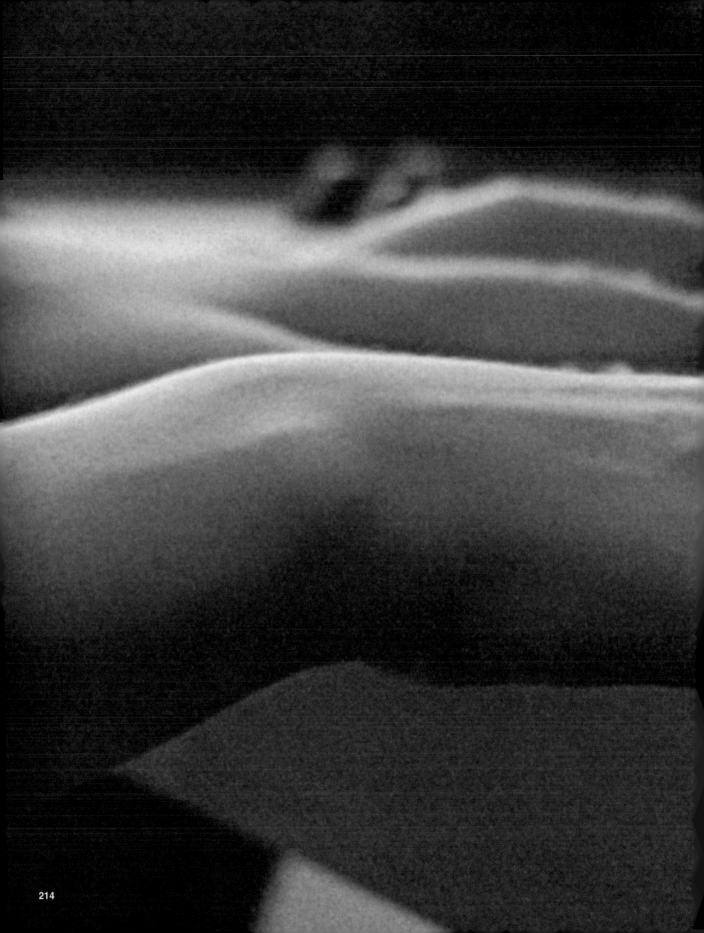

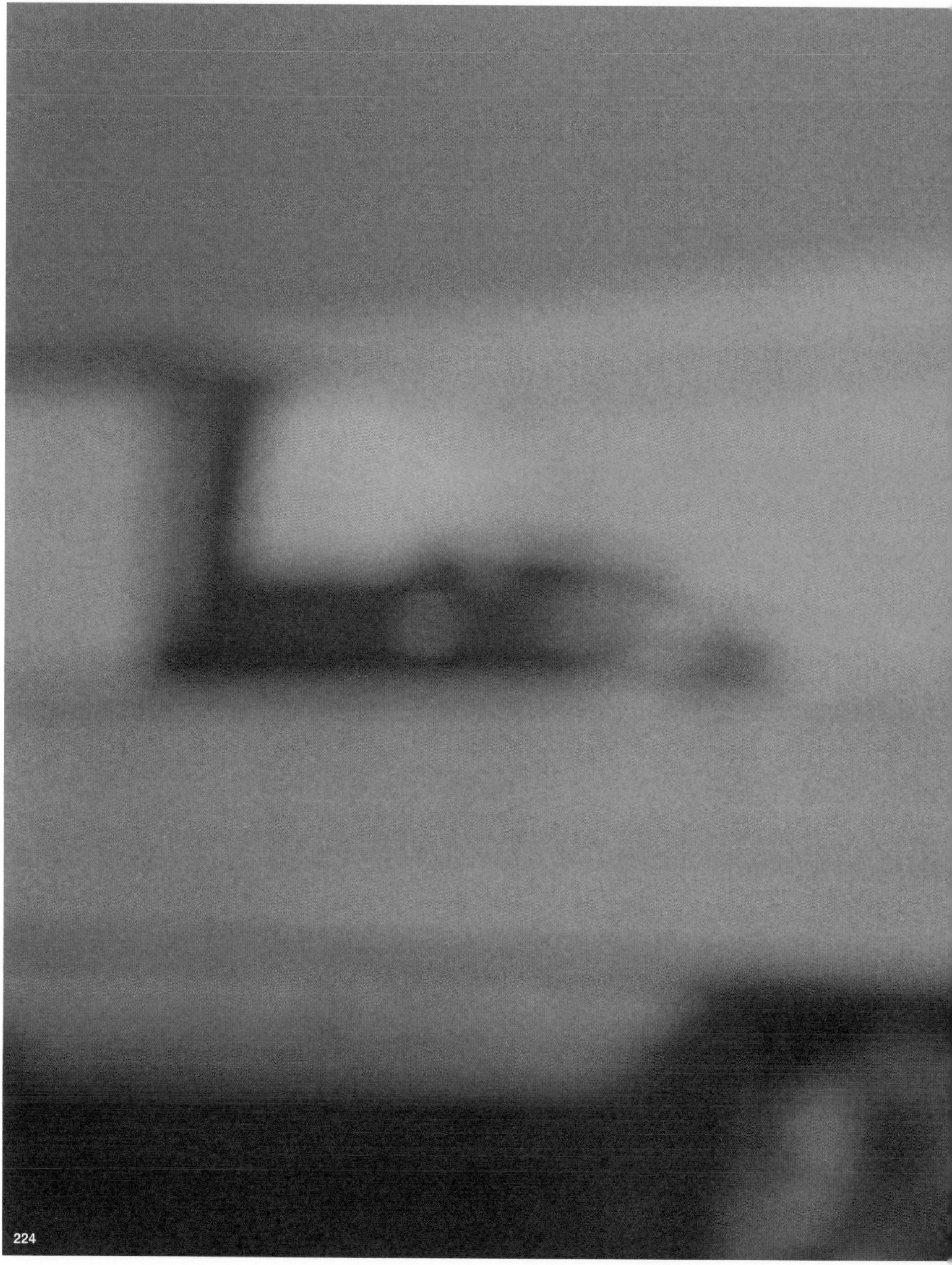

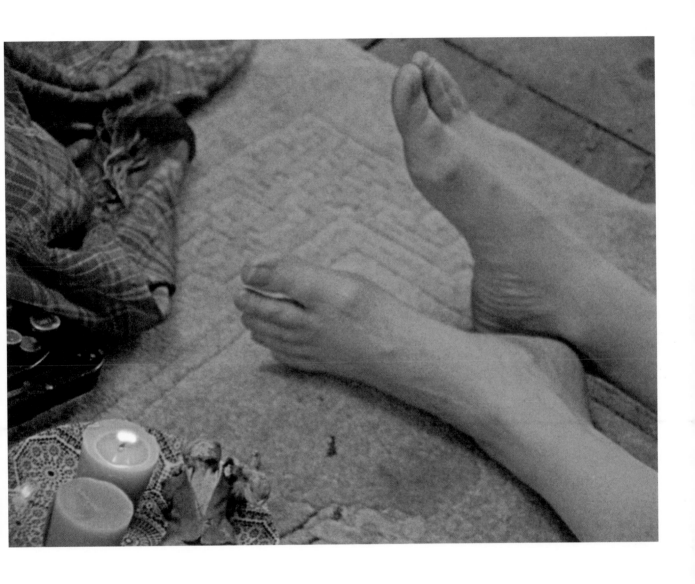

241

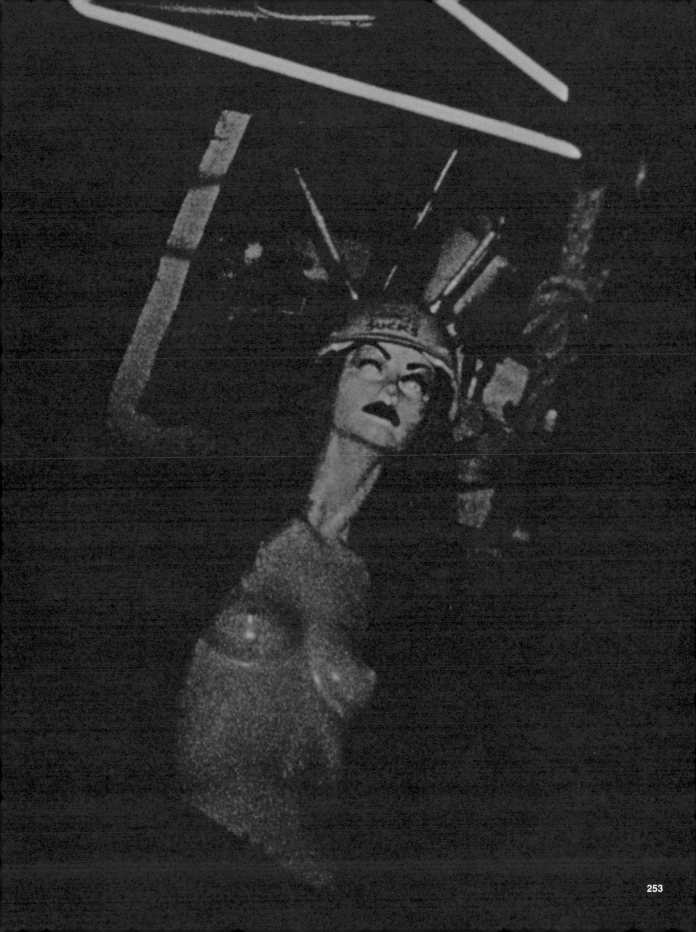

When in the course of human events
it becomes necessary
for one people to dissolve the political bands
which have connected them with another,
and to assume among the powers of the earth,
the separate and equal station to which
the Laws of Nature and of Nature's God entitle them,
a decent respect to the opinions of mankind
requires that they should declare the causes
which impel them to the separation.
We hold these truths to be self-evident,
that all men are created equal,
that they are endowed by their creator
with certain unalienable Rights,
that among these are Life, Liberty and the pursuit
of Happiness.
– That to secure these rights, Governments are
instituted among Men, deriving their just powers
from the consent of the governed.
– That whenever any Form of Government becomes
destructive to those ends,
it is the Right of the People to alter or to abolish it.

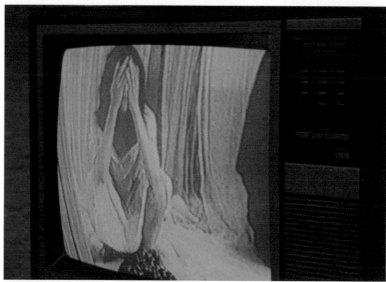

This was my favorite dress
when I was a little girl.
I just loved this dress.
It's one of the few things I have left
of my childhood,
but I can see my whole childhood
in this one little dress.
It's hand...it's homemade.
Anyway, it's a nice little thing.

When one loses someone that's extremely important, it does alter one, but not necessarily for the bad. I mean losing my brother, for instance, who I was extremely close with, completely adored, and he was so encouraging to me since our childhood. I was a bit older than him, but he always made me feel special. When he died, after the initial shock which was terrible, because he wasn't...it was sudden. I actually, since then, have felt like I'm a better person because my heart really was filled with my brother after he died. I mean I literally, my heart went from feeling like a cold black ember to a warm, really joyful flame, and I almost every day you know thinking about him, he always makes me smile. I mean I...I still... I mean I always miss him and everything, and sometimes it, you know, I can access the pain of missing him, but I can say that I'm a more optimistic person. All his finest qualities somehow entered me as a human being when he died.

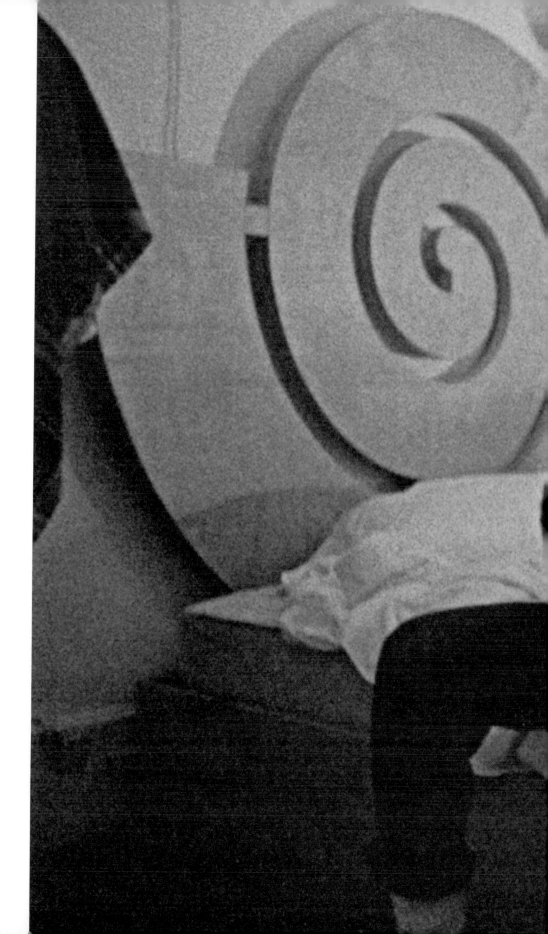

POLAROIDS

BY

PATTI SMITH

MOMENTS CAPTURED
1996 – 2007

(DURING THE PERIOD OF FILMING *DREAM OF LIFE*)

CHILDHOOD DRESS. NEW YORK, 2006

ARTHUR RIMBAUD'S FORK AND SPOON. CHARLEVILLE-MEZIERES, FRANCE, 2005

FRED SONIC SMITH'S GRAVE. DETROIT, 2004

FLOWERS BACKSTAGE ON CBGB'S FINAL NIGHT. NEW YORK, 2006

CENTRAL PARK. NEW YORK, 2007

JESSE SMITH. STRAWBERRY FIELDS, CENTRAL PARK, NEW YORK, 2007

GREGORY CORSO'S GRAVE. CEMETERY ACATTOLICO, ROME, ITALY, 2002

WILLIAM BLAKE'S GRAVE. BUNHILL FIELDS CEMETERY, LONDON, 2005

PORTRAIT OF DIRECTOR STEVEN SEBRING. NEW YORK, 2006

FINAL CLOSING NIGHT OF CBGB'S. NEW YORK, 2006

PATTI'S GUITAR IN HER BEDROOM. NEW YORK, 2007

GARDEN WALL OF ARTHUR RIMBAUD. CHARLEVILLE-MEZIERES, FRANCE, 2005

PERCY BYSSHE SHELLEY'S GRAVE. CEMETERY ACATTOLICO, ROME, ITALY, 2002

STRANGE MESSENGER IN PROGRESS. NEW YORK, 2004

HANDMADE TAMBOURINE BY ROBERT MAPPLETHORPE. NEW YORK, 2006

313

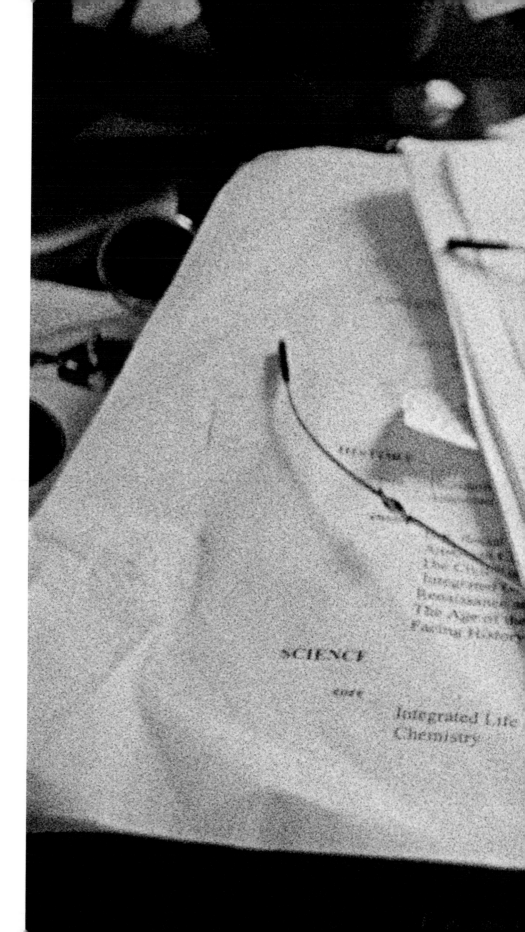

This is about the preservation of our planet.
We have to join forces.
We cannot have war.
There is no righteous war.
We must do that.
We must get activated.
We must use our numbers.

And to institute a new Government,
laying its foundation on such principles
and organizing its powers in such form
as to them shall seem most likely
to effect their Safety and their Happiness...

But when a long train of abuses...
it is their right, it is their right,
it is their duty, to throw off such Government.

He has suspended the rights of American citizens to
fundamental civil liberties.
He has forgotten that the United States was founded on the
proposition of the separation of church and state. We...
we indict George W. Bush for befouling our country's name.
For using the rhetoric of freedom to justify tyranny,
for rigging the election process,
for squandering a vast federal surplus while giving
tax breaks to the rich,
for forsaking the poor,
for ignoring internal,
international agreements to protect the environment,
for abandoning Alaska to the oil companies,
for abandoning New Orleans,
for depriving prisoners of the benefits of a trial by jury,
for establishing secret prisons on foreign soil,
for authorizing illegal eavesdropping and surveillance,
for waging a war based on lies.
We indict George W. Bush.

The typewriter is holy, the poem is holy,
the hearers are holy, the ecstasy is holy!
Holy Peter, holy Allen, holy Solomon, holy Lucien,
holy Kerouac, holy Huncke, holy Burroughs, holy Cassady,
holy the unknown buggered and suffering beggars,
holy the hideous human angels,
holy my mother in the insane asylum,
holy the cocks of the grandfathers of Kansas!
Holy the groaning saxophone!
Holy the bop apocalypse!
Holy the jazz bands, marijuana hipsters, peace and junk and drums!
Holy the solitudes of skyscrapers and pavements!
Holy the cafeterias filled with the millions!
Holy the mysterious rivers of tears under the streets!
Holy the lone juggernaut!
Holy the vast lamb of the middle class!
Holy! Ours! Bodies! Suffering! Magnanimity!
Holy the supernatural, extra-brilliant, intelligent kindness of the soul!

VIETNAM TOUR

conrad speaks   of darkness   the day

journey   what of it   is it beauty   the heart as

ry no race no BODY of thought   Free   and our inner

one moment where we belong to none and no

ng for one is born free at least for a breath

RNEY is a state of mind and a stateless souls

NAM is the growing pains of youth

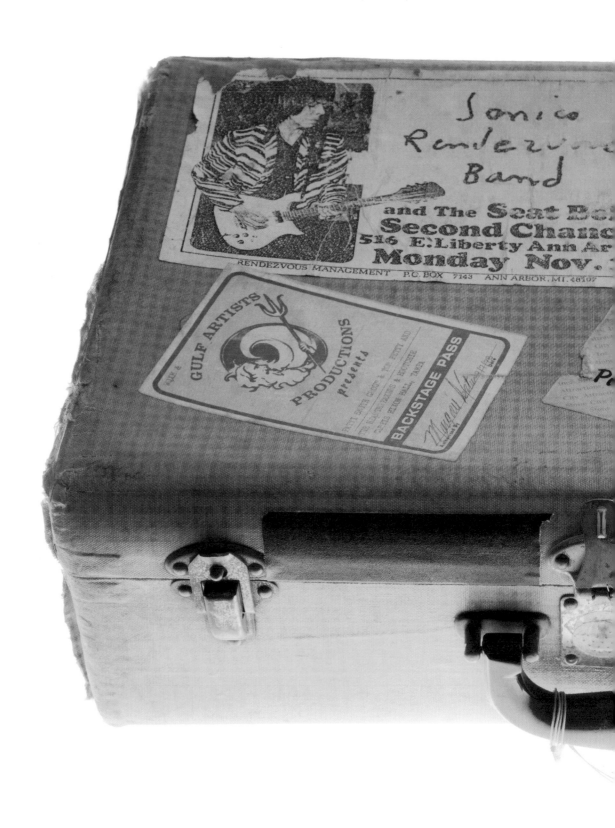

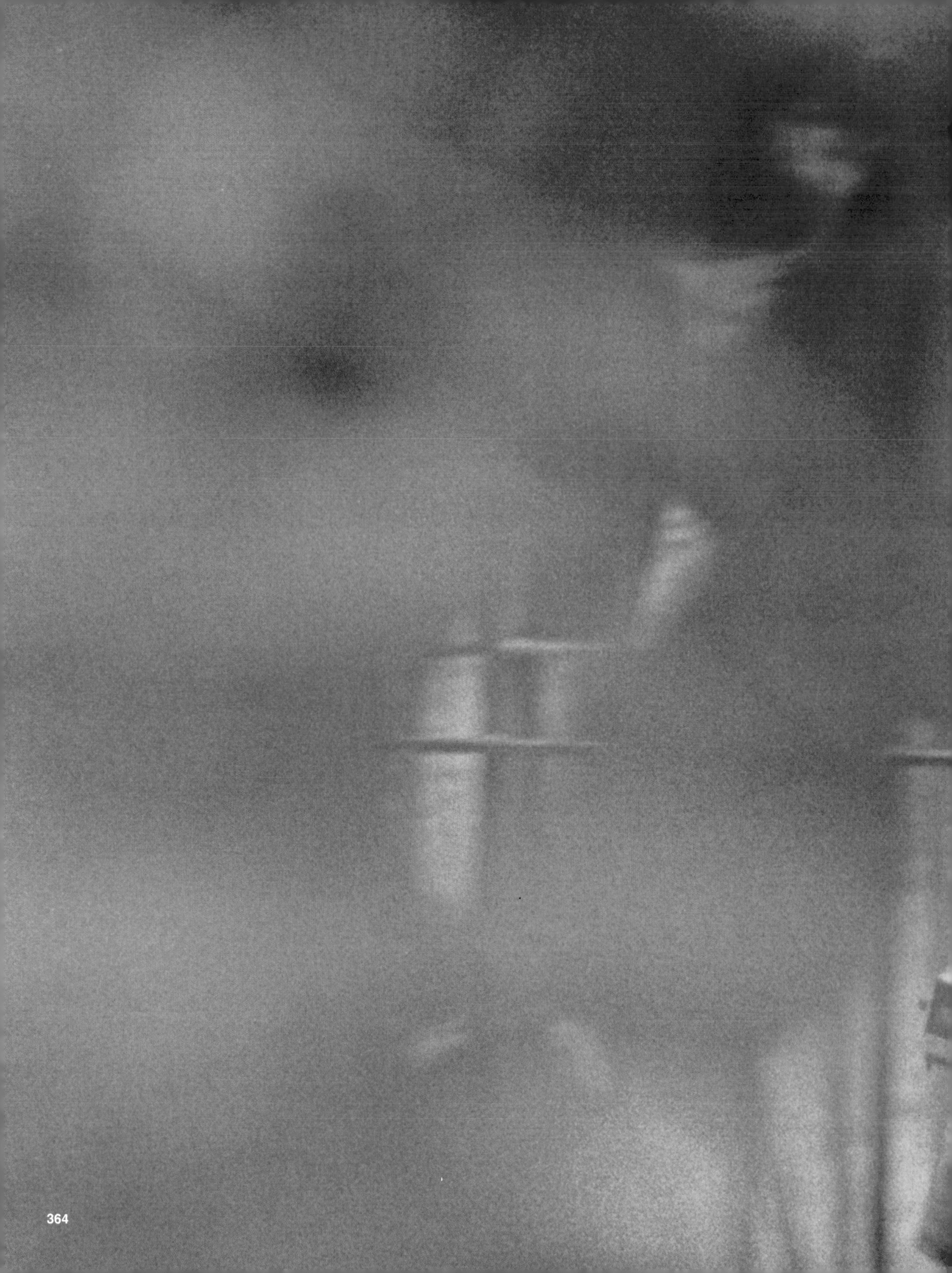

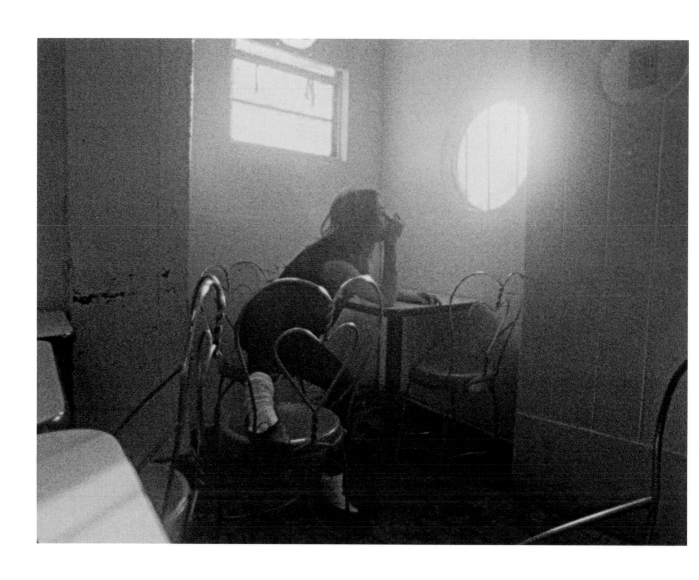

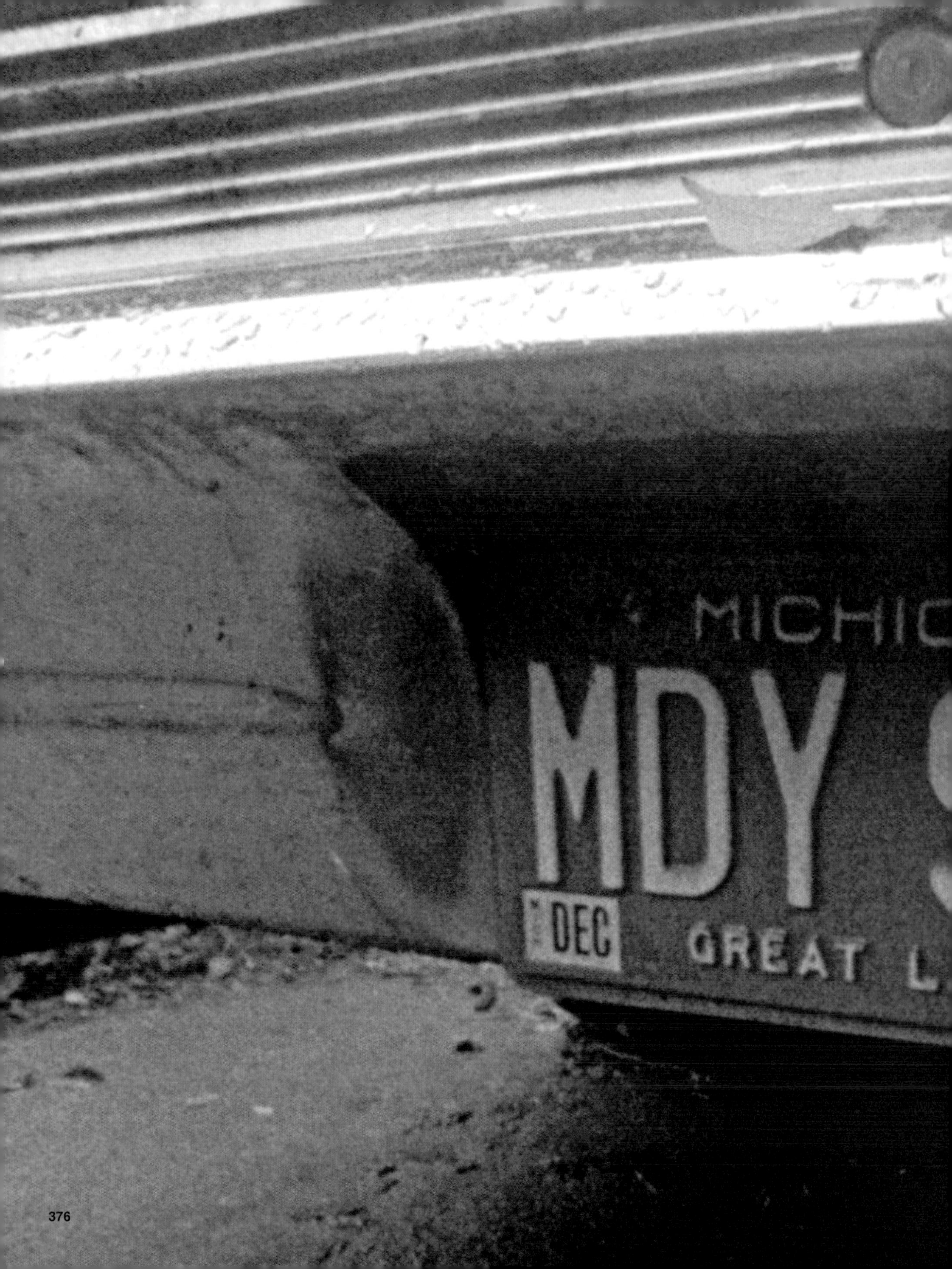
MICHIG
MDY S
DEC
GREAT L

Robert and I did this little movie,
Still Moving,
did you ever see it?
Well, we did it in '78 I think.
It's black and white.
I don't know what mill...it's probably 16 millimeter.
But I did the soundtrack music for it.
It wasn't as good as this but...it was in the realm,
and it just made me think of that.

Look, two hot dogs, two dollars.

Robert loved Nathan's, Robert and I used to go
to Coney Island all the time.
We'd go all the way to Coney Island just to get a
Nathan's hot dog.
He just loved them so much.

R BY LIE THE REMAINS OF

THE POET-PAINTER

WILLIAM BLAKE

1757 — 1827

AND OF HIS WIFE

CATHERINE SOPHIA

17

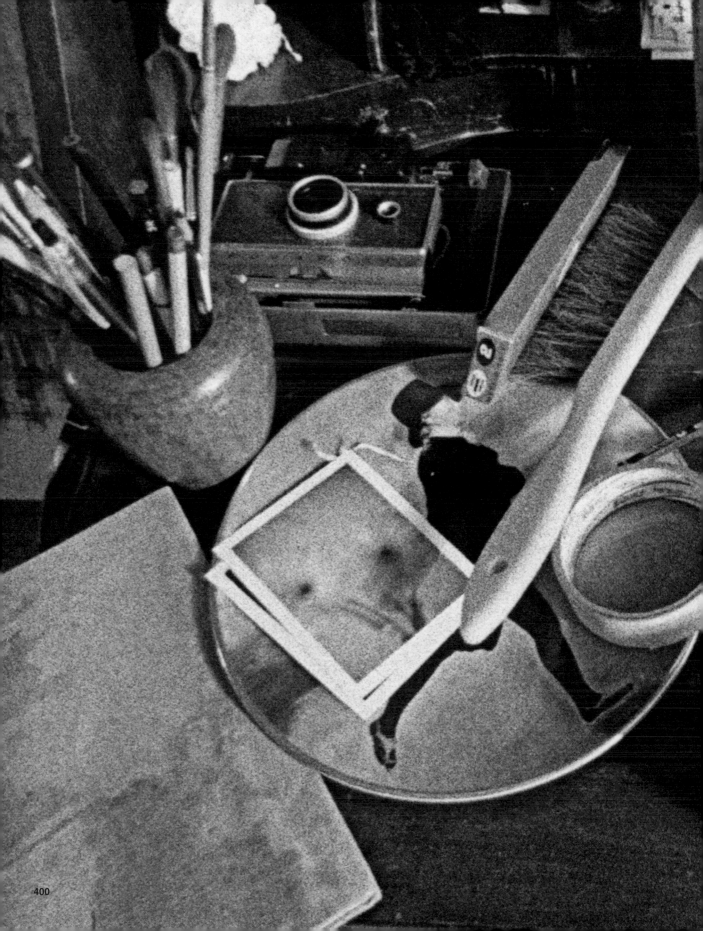

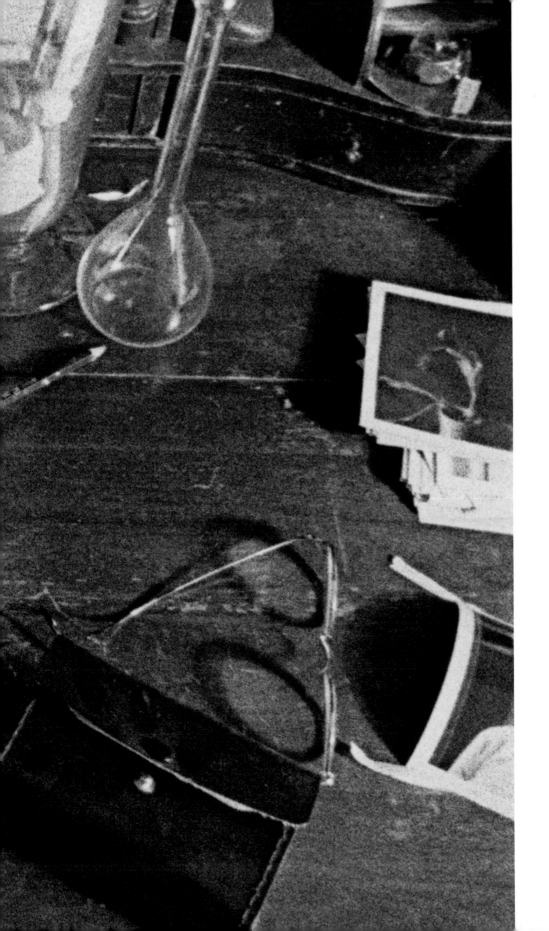

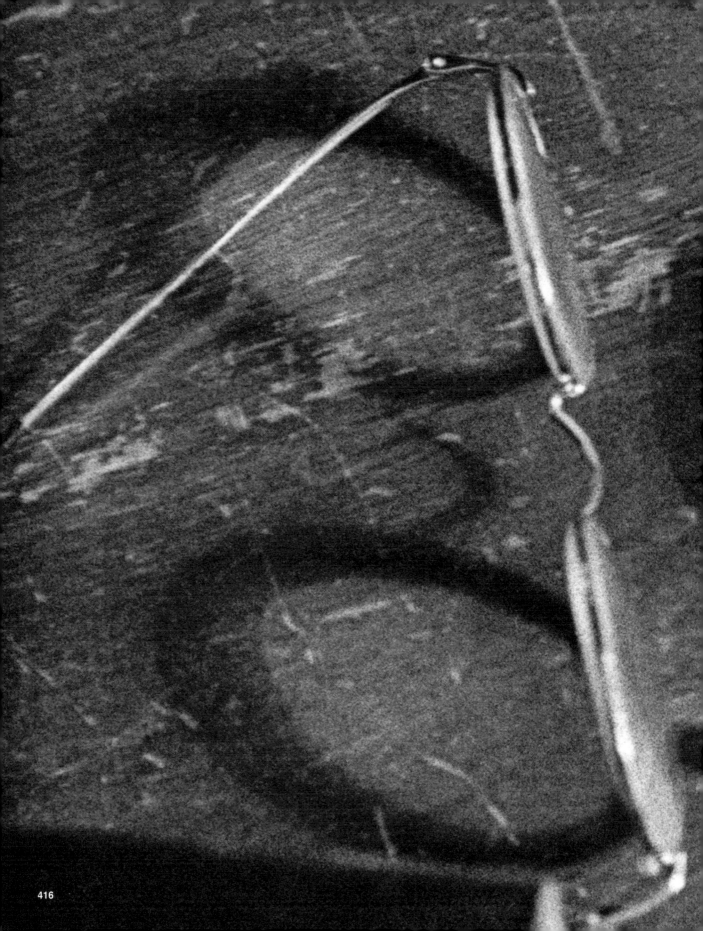

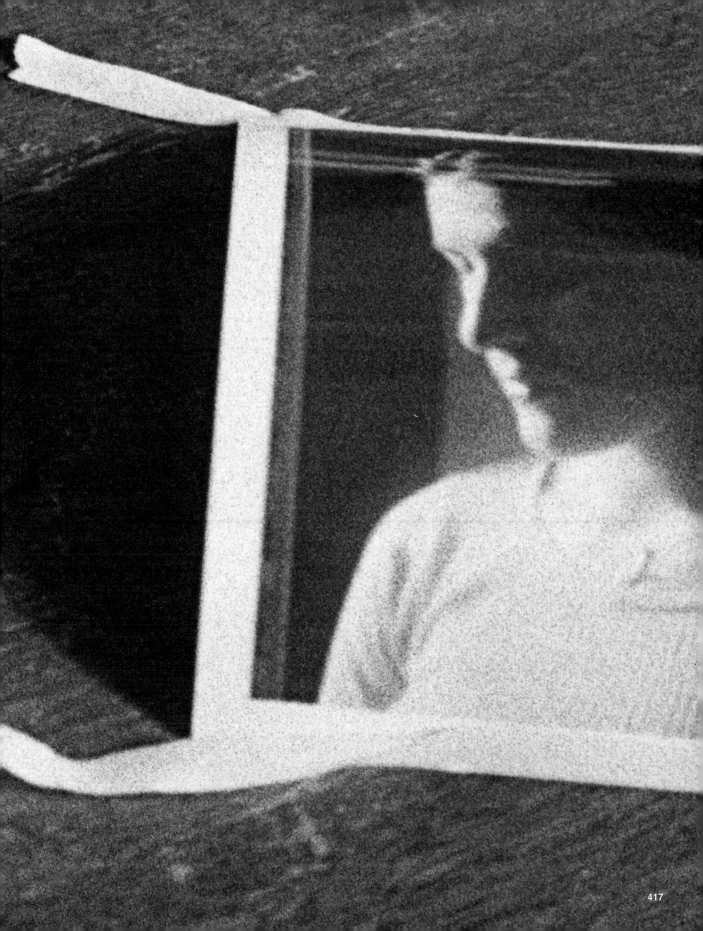

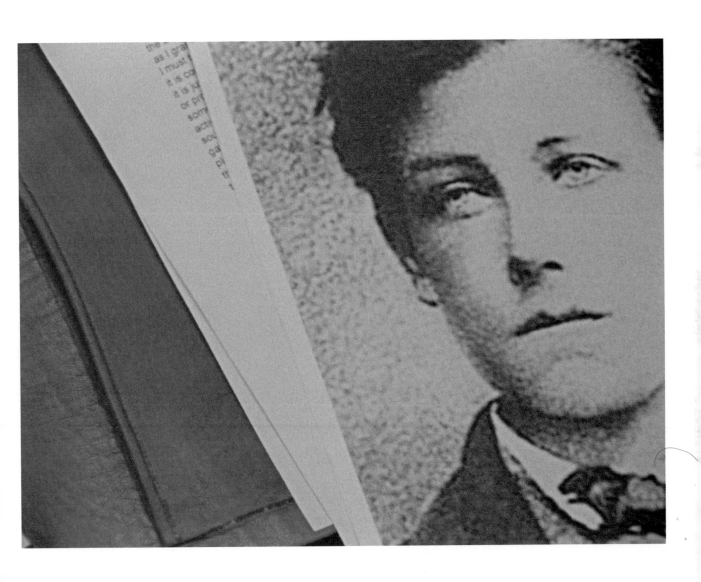

419

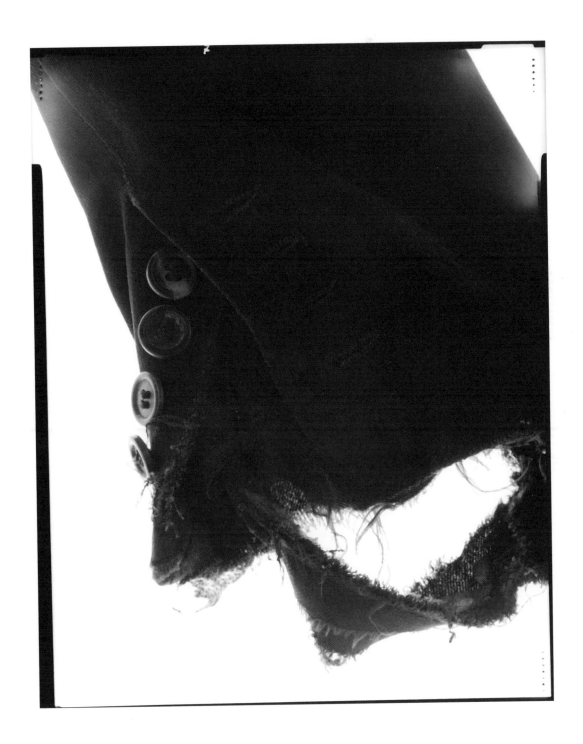

427

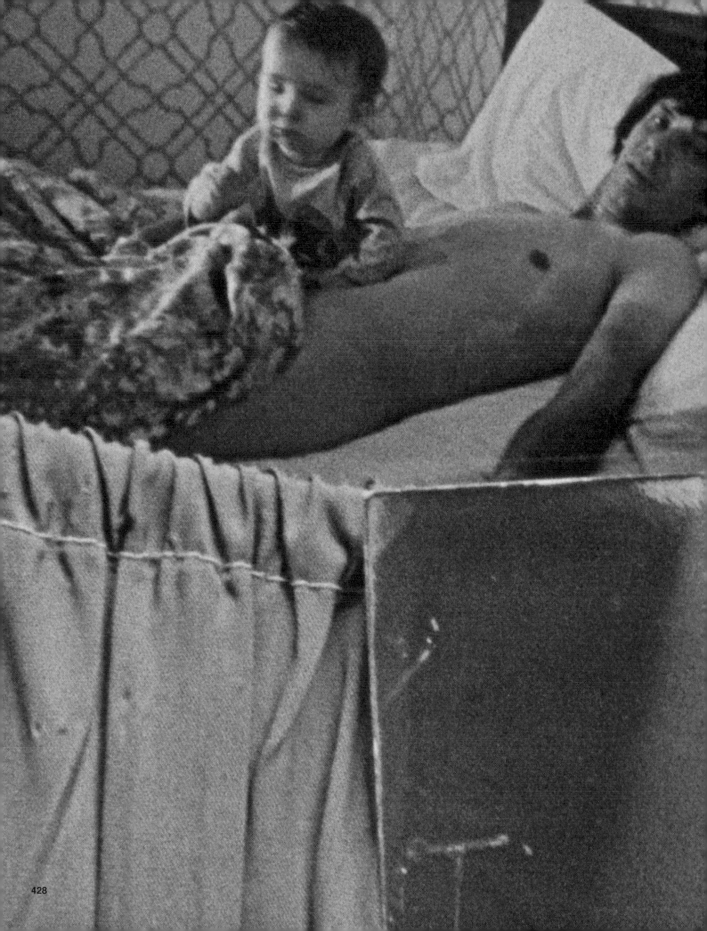

429

Index

431

First published in the United States of America in 2008
by RIZZOLI INTERNATIONAL PUBLICATIONS, INC.
300 Park Avenue South
New York, NY 10010
www.rizzoliusa.com

© 2008 Rizzoli International Publications, Inc.
Photographs © 2008 Steven Sebring
Photographs © 2008 Patti Smith

Art Direction & Design:
Alex Wiederin, Sylvia Gruber / Buero New York

ISBN-13: 978-0-8478-3208-8
Library of Congress Control Number: 2008930941

Per l'edizione italiana:
© 2008 RCS Libri Spa, Milano
Tutti i diritti riservati
www.rizzoli.eu

ISBN 978-88-1702682-6

Traduzione: Franco Zanetti
Redazione: Chiara Ratti

Stampato in Cina